W9-AUA-842

VOCAL FREEDOM

Music is a healing art, the voice its magic life.

Suzanne Kiechle
Vocal Coach • Voice Teacher • Voice Repair

MARKWIN PRESS

Silver Springs, Nevada

First Edition copyright© 2008 Suzanne Kiechle

All rights reserved. No part of this publication may
Be produced, stored in a retrieval system or
Transmitted in any form or by any means,
electronic, mechanical, photocopying, recording
or otherwise, without the prior written permission
of the publisher.

Library of Congress Catalog Number 2008936564
ISBN 0-9740793-3-2
ISBN 13: 978-0-9740793-3-2

Published b y Markwin Press, Nevada
Editor: Katy Kerris
Design and Illustrations:
Ann Thompson

Printed in the United States of America

FORWARD

You will find in this volume a healthy approach to obtaining and maintaining vocal function. It contains a distillation of the mechanisms required to provide the technical ability to sing without interfering with the art of music.

Voice is essentially a natural form of expression and as long as we exploit our natural abilities without resorting to artificial gestures and inappropriate muscle use, it is also durable.

Suzanne's concepts are accurate and have stood the test of time with vocalist after vocalist. Proper mechanisms of support, correct placement along with enjoying the ability to sing are the keys to a productive career.

Charles Schneider, D.D.S., M.D.
Otorhinolaryngologist

INTRODUCTION
By John Rubinstein

When I had my first lesson with Suzanne Kiechle, I was in horrible shape. I was three months into a year-long contract to act and sing a role that was extremely demanding, vocally and physically, in a musical eight times a week. My voice suddenly quit on me in the middle of a performance. I was diagnosed as having a nodule on my vocal cord, and ordered to remain completely silent for three weeks. The doctor gave me two options: the node might disappear on its own, but I would most likely have to remain out of the show until that happened. If it didn't, I would require surgery, and much longer hiatus from the show, not to mention the potential risks of the operation itself. After the three weeks of total silence, the node was still there.

Not quite believing it possible, I came to Suzanne hoping she could help me try a third option: to continue in the show and help my nodule disappear simultaneously. So simple and straightforward is Suzanne's teaching, that after only one session with her I was able to change, in a very fundamental way, my entire approach to singing in the theatre. That very night I stood on stage, my voice in ragged condition, and belted out my show using her techniques as far as I'd been able to absorb them in one lesson. At the end of the show, not only was my voice not tired as usual, it actually felt and sounded better than it had at the start of the evening! After a few more sessions with Suzanne, the raggedness disappeared, my stamina and confidence returned and then redoubled. People who had known me for years, and who had seen and heard me in this very show some months before, began to show up backstage saying that the sound I was now producing was stronger, richer, more musical, even in the higher register. I was able to play my role and actually enjoy singing the songs, interpreting them as I was moved to do, rather than simply trying to get away without a noticeable squeak or strain.

I continued in the same role for another ten months, and never missed another performance. Even when I had a cold or sore throat, Suzanne's exercises and performance methods helped me to over come the disabilities and sing well without injuring myself. And, most important of all, even with all those performances of frequent, loud, and emotional singing, the nodule on my vocal cord disappeared completely, and stayed gone!

Dedication

I dedicate this book to my mother, Anne Beatrice Connor Kiechle, who gave me life and a great love for music and the voice. My mother was a fine pianist and sang beautifully up until she died at 86. The last song she sang was "*The hills are alive, with the sound of music.*" She would burst into that phrase in elevators and while she was in bed at the convalescent home. Amazingly, with all her illness, her voice was strong and beautiful.

My mother, often called Auntie Bea by our friends, was my choir director and music teacher in grammar school. She taught me how to play piano. When I took trumpet lessons, she accompanied me on the piano. Musically, she was technically correct while playing with feeling and passion. She studied as a youngster in Pittsburgh with Maria Caveney who studied at the Sorbonne in France. My mother was proud of her French influences, which were often recognized by other French musicians.

Chopin, Debussy, Rachmaninoff, the 2nd Piano Concerto…I would play the orchestral part and she would play the piano part, then we would switch. She was always technically better than I was but we enjoyed the music together. How lucky I was to have so much music in my life. Not only did she take me to the many lessons I had, but she supported all my musical endeavors, including the Music Academy of the West in Santa Barbara, and the Los Angeles Junior Philharmonic. She played the piano for the shows done at our Parish Church, conducted the children's choir, and accompanied the High School Choir with Lucienne Biggs as conductor.

The value of the release of breath became clear when my mother had an emergency visit to her cardiologist. We were in the examining room and a couple of nurses came to take her vital signs and give her an EKG. Her breathing was labored. The nurses left the room and Mom and I were alone to wait for the doctor. Mother's breathing was increasingly difficult. I was very scared, so I started to sing her a lullaby she had taught me—*"Baby boat's a silver moon, sailing through the sky.   Sailing on a sea of dreams, while the clouds roll by."* She started to sing with me and her breathing restored to normal. She even corrected me on one of the words. Tears were streaming down my face in one of the magic moments of my life. We kept singing until the doctor arrived.

Music is a healing art, the voice its magic life.
How blessed we all are to be able to express ourselves through the magic of our voices.

Thank you, Mom, for that gift.

Table of Contents

Chapter 1
Understanding the Language

The most difficult thing in writing this book is the vocabulary. Words mean different things to different people. I am not going to be understood in the way I wish by everyone. I, too, am guilty of jumping to conclusions about other voice teachers' explanations of how the voice works. In discussing issues with friends who seem to have different views, when it comes down to it, we want the same thing but have different ideas on how to get there.

Most voice teachers want their students to sing freely. My teacher talked in ways of power more than freedom. I ended up with nodes. My mission is to communicate in the best way I can on how to be vocally free to sing any kind of music and in speech, to be free to make whatever sounds you wish without damaging the voice.

It is a tricky thing to be clear in language. In this book I strive to present concepts in an understandable way, and to keep discussions on anatomy simple. Other books and references go into the complex anatomy of vocal production. This is not my aim. In my teaching, students understand what I am saying by keeping things simple.

As we travel through this vocal experience, get comfortable. Take off your shoes, lie down, relax and breathe.

Chapter 2
The Keys to Vocal Freedom

Within these pages are the keys to vocal freedom. If you choose to take this journey to freeing your voice, be patient and enjoy the process of letting go. If you follow the path laid out, you will be vocally unrestricted. You will get the most from your vocal instrument - endurance, flexibility, tone enhancement, richness—for any style of music or any vocal sounds you have to make. You will produce sound in a safe manner for the structures of the vocal instrument.

How long will it take? It depends how quickly you can let go of bad habits and learn new habits. Remember, it took time for the bad habits to develop. This is your one and only voice, and it is worth the time and effort put into its development. Commit yourself to improving and growing safely with a technique that will keep you vocally healthy and free. With diligence, your journey will be smooth and your outcome quick.

I was given the keys when I was 30 years old by my otorhinolaryngologist, Dr. Charles Schneider. I was teaching high school and rehearsing all afternoon and evening with a professional singing group preparing for a big audition. I developed vocal nodes. I was vocally fried and scared to death I wouldn't be able to do the audition, which was in a couple of days. Dr. Schneider assured me I could get rid of the nodes before the audition. He told me I didn't breathe properly when I spoke. I attribute it to run-on sentences and the California back of the throat way of talking.

The technical problems were improper breath support, forming the words with the back of the tongue, causing tension in the larynx and stress on the vocal folds.

I don't remember what I actually changed at the time, except that I used the breath more effectively. When he told me I could get rid of the nodes and sing fine, the fear went away, allowing the breath to flow.

Study the following pages, full of information on vocal anatomy in layman's terms. There are common problems stated with clear solutions. These pages contain hands-on activities and exercises to help you understand the tips for vocal production. I have included true case studies to illustrate points. This handbook is designed to be user friendly

No matter what you teach about singing, you can take the information in this book and use it to increase the value of what you teach. This vocal technique is very specific and it fits all uses of the voice and all styles of music. Everyone has different ways they hear sound, and how the tone is interpreted. Beyond the tone and musicality of the singer comes the mechanics in making the tones. In this book I am dealing with the mechanics and the effects on vocal production. When there is not enough breath for the pitch, there is stress on the vocal folds.

In teaching voice we are dealing with an instrument we cannot see unlike a flute where we can see the lips blowing into it. With singing we can see the external equipment, lips, tongue, jaw, abdominal movement and the front of the larynx. But without an endoscope we cannot see inside the larynx.

Besides my years of work with Dr. Charles Schneider using an endoscope, I spent seven days in Philadelphia looking at videos and listening to Laryngologists, Phonosurgeons, Speech Pathologists and Voice Teachers from all over the world.

I had many conversations with the professionals I met, mostly voice teachers, who wanted to know the latest in medical discoveries.

At one of the afternoon seminars, a voice teacher asked about pitch. The answer had to do with measuring vibrations which truly did not address the question in a practical way. I raised my hand and said "when the pitch is flat, the back of the tongue is depressed down and there is not enough breath for the pitch and when the pitch is sharp the back of the tongue is forced up. When the tongue is relaxed and the sound is at the roof of the mouth, it is in tune." I got no response except from the woman who asked the question. There was not an expert on the panel who truly knew the answer. I actually heard a voice teacher, with a PhD ask one of the experts if I was right. I responded when I heard that question and said, " Try it! That is the only way you will know if my information is correct."

That evening Kristin Linklater, who wrote the book, **FREEING THE NATURAL VOICE**, spoke. She talked about that afternoons symposium and quoted me saying, "a woman stood up and said, "when the back of the tongue" etc. she completely quoted me and then said "she answered the question and you acted like, isn't that nice." She was really chastising them for not acknowledging my explanation as the answer to the question.

This International Voice Conference was held in 1996 and Doctor Schneider had taught me about the vocal instrument in 1974. The information he gave me changed my whole life of singing. Luckily I was sent to Dr. Schneider by my voice teacher when I had nodes. I never took another voice lesson. As much as I loved my voice teacher, I realized he didn't understand how the voice worked even though he had pictures of the vocal anatomy on his walls. He was a concert pianist who accompanied a famous voice teacher at the

Metropolitan Opera House and took over for the voice
teacher who had become ill.

Chapter 3
The Beginning

What is something we do everyday, automatically? Did you say breathe? Without breath, there is no life, so why is there so much confusion about breathing when you're singing?

There are many theories about singing, but knowing how to use the breath is the most important factor for healthy singing. Activating the diaphragm pulls the breath into the lungs, and then lifting or moving the abdominals propels air out of the lungs and over/through the structures that create the sound. When students have learned other ways of breathing there is tension on the larynx and/or vocal cords and vocal function is diminished. I have had many successes in repairing vocal injury, and they are all based on teaching proper breathing while singing.

Do we naturally use our breath correctly? When we are babies, yes. Our little bellies are going in and out as we yell and our diaphragms are pushing up and propelling the air and sound out. Babies are loud, and I've never heard one with laryngitis.

As we get older, we begin holding the tummy in to look better or to support our backs when we exercise. We stop using the power source of active abdominal muscles to support the voice.

Place your hands on your belly. As you breathe in, you should feel the belly moving out. As you breathe out, the belly moves in. This is the natural way most people breathe, and is the basis for what I am talking about. For some people, the movement of the belly is not natural. They have developed a muscle memory of breathing in an inefficient way. With practice, it is possible to return the pattern of breathing to the more natural and efficient way and then begin pairing it with vocal production.

When I was beginning my career as a voice teacher, a student confronted me. "Why does your voice always sound hoarse when you're speaking about keeping the throat relaxed?" To change my own habit of speaking in the back of my throat, I gave myself a month where I thought about it and made the change, sending breath through the throat and attaching words as the sound came forward. I did it by sighing and speaking through the sigh, expelling the breath by using the abdominals and relaxing my throat and tongue. I quit sucking my breath in and raising my chest on the inhale and began to breathe silently, removing strain from my structures.

You, too, can have better vocal health by following the instructions on the following pages. Learn how to breathe properly and never get lazy about it. It is the one activity that will keep you vocally healthy.

Chapter 4
The Breath

Every movement of the voice should be done with the breath. Breath vibrates the vocal folds and carries vibration/sound through the larynx, vibrating off the spine and moving forward over the tongue, vibrating at the roof of the mouth, then through the lips, which form the words. Breath is the life and energy source that creates the sound and carries it to the universe.

Problem:
The "sucky" breath. If a singer uses the throat muscles to bring the breath in, it makes a sucked in sound. Sucking the breath in pulls the larynx down and the vocal folds out of position for singing and speaking, causing tension on the vocal structures.

Putting weight on vocal structures causes tension and a struggle for breath to come in and vibrate the cords. It is like doing ballet in combat boots. The habit of sucking in the breath has a snowball effect on vocal function. The throat gets tighter and tighter, the voice more strained, the sound thinner, and this can lead to vocal cord injury.

Solution:
Breathing should be silent. This one correction can make a huge difference for a healthy functioning voice.

Problem:
Students complain of a feeling of dryness in the throat.

Solution:
The folds need moisture to vibrate freely, just like the lips need moisture when playing an instrument like trumpet, flute, or clarinet. Woodwind instruments require a moist reed to vibrate. Dry structures are stiff structures. If you breathe correctly, with no sucking of the breath on inhalation, you can keep the moisture in the vocal structure. Staying hydrated involves drinking water, and using nasal sprays that are just saline solutions.

There are also anti-bacterial gels to keep the moisture in and the germs out. The Doctor can recommend nasal salves for nasal hydration. Take a cup with very hot water, and sniff the steam (do not let your nose touch the hot water; just sniff up the steam). For singers who are on the road, bring a thermos and always have hot water available for the dressing room and backstage. A humidifier is also helpful. Being in the dry climate of Los Angeles, CA., I use a humidifier in my studio.

Problem:
Students stop and drop the note, keeping the air from moving forward. This causes the sound to fall back in the throat. Singers tend to drop the forward motion of the breath on the last note of a phrase. It is fatiguing for the vocal folds to be suspended and vibrating, and then to lose support of the breath. The vocal folds drop down into resting position in the larynx and then have to be raised into activity by the breath. It is easy to get

sloppy about the timing of the forward movement of the breath if the energy is dropped.

Solution:
Don't drop when you stop. Learn to continuously use the breath, carrying the sound over the tongue, brushing the roof of the mouth, and going out the lips. Avoid interference from the base of the tongue. To

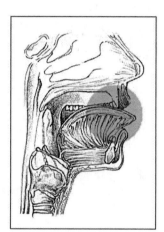

make a staccato word within the phrase for dramatic effect, end the word with the breath moving forward, making sure the tongue doesn't get in the way of the breath. Start the sound forward, keep it going forward and end the sound forward out your lips.

Problem:
Singers who perform on stage often move during a song. Sometimes the required movement causes tension in the vocal structures, which through repetition can lead to vocal injury.

Solution:
Choreograph the breath into the song. Just like the performer is staged, or directed to move from one position to another, the breath action needs to be planned into the song, choreographing the movement of the abdominals with the notes and words to send out

the sound in a relaxed manner. Higher notes, louder sounds, accented and sustained notes, all require varying degrees of air pressure to do the job. Both abdominal movement and the squeezing of your buttocks, help to make the required movement for a given pitch. It sounds like a lot to think about, but with practice connecting the breath with the movements it becomes second nature, allowing the performer to have fun and freedom without vocal damage.

Problem:
Professional speakers and actors must project their sound. Hesitating, as in making sure you are answering a question well, often backs up the breath, putting the words in the back of the throat.

Solution:
Give the support the folds need and deserve. Vocal folds want to perform at their best but they need to be supported all the time. Practice expelling breath through the throat and attaching words to the breath with the front of the tongue and lips. Hum, vibrating the lips and speak through the hum.

Problem:
Vibrato can be forced by a singer "holding the note" in the back of the throat, putting pressure on the larynx and the back of the tongue.
Tight vibrato can make the jaw shake and the larynx waver, even to the viewer's eye. What we are seeing is tension.

Solution:

Lift the soft palate (top of the yawn) sending the sound to the roof of the mouth and causing it to echo back and forth like the reverberation of singing in a shower or a cathedral. Some singers have a natural, healthy vibrato, where there is not

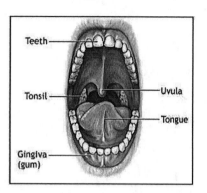

shaking of the jaw, head, stomach, or larynx. With a straight tone, or no vibrato, the breath drives the tone straight out of the mouth.

Problem:

Fast vibrato can be a forced vibrato and be injurious to the voice. A slow, sagging, or wide vibrato can stress the vocal folds by spreading them or "sitting on them" putting negative pressure on the folds.

Solution:

Instead of driving the sound through the mouth, raise the air pressure and allow the sound to ring under the roof of your mouth. Let the sound "hang out" for a few seconds in your mouth, as if you are tasting a good wine.

A healthy vibrato is not fast, or slow, but right in the middle. Palpate the larynx. If it is relaxed, not shaking, pushed down, or wide, it is

probably fine. You will feel the vibrations while palpating; and vibrations are good and necessary. It is the stress upon ending the sound, when the structure drops quickly (what I call a snap) that is tension.

Problem:
Closing the mouth too soon at the end of a phrase shuts off the flow of air. This tightens the larynx, the cricoid cartilage blocks the opening, and the vocal folds drop.

Solution:
Don't close the mouth until the sound is finished. You can end the word after you have stopped the sound. This is a subtle but effective way to avoid the problem of closing the mouth too soon and causing the breath to back up, the vocal folds to drop, and the larynx to lower. The breath must be moved forward at all times carrying the sound out the lips.

Try This:
1. To take a silent breath, open your mouth and expand your abdominals (belly button area). The diaphragm pulls down, creating negative pressure in the lungs, and the air rushes in 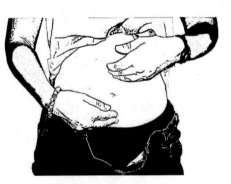 without a sound and without tension on the vocal structure. Tightening the abdominals sends the air up and out, allowing for free singing.

2. Take your fingers and press on the spine at the back of the neck. Hum, and you will feel vibration.
The more forward the sound, the more vibration you will feel, especially in the lower register. On high notes, you will feel the energy moving.

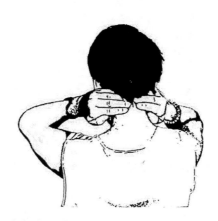

3. Drop your jaw, relaxing the tongue, keeping the tip at the back of the bottom teeth and out of the way of the breath. On inhalation, expand the abdominals, and the diaphragm goes down. With exhalation, lift the abdominals propelling the air out of the lungs.

Case Study:

Vocal exercises can help heal nodes, take the stress off the vocal folds, and get circulation going to allow for healing. If the cause of the injury is due to performance, rehearsal, or recording, vocal behavior must be changed. This is where choreographing the breath is essential to vocal health.

I worked with a leading lady in the musical *"Showboat"*. She had one number where she was singing and dancing at the same time. She got a node on her vocal cords on the pitch of C# an octave above middle C. When I went to see the show, I noticed at first she sounded fine, but at the point of the C#, she made a turn, twirling a parasol. I heard her throat tighten at that point and the notes following the C# were not clear. When she came in for her next lesson, I had her do the move for me as she sang and told her to bring in her abdominals, choreographing the breath with the dance movement and the C#. Problem solved, the node was history. It was the repeated motion, the lack of breath support at that particular point in the performance, night after night in the three year run that caused the node.

Remember:
● Use the diaphragm and the abdominal muscles to breathe.

● A stress-free breath is silent.

● Good use of the breath is the key that unlocks the voice and places the sound so it travels easily out the lips.

Chapter 5
Choreographing the Breath

Planning where in a song you need to send up the breath is the key. Which notes require more breath to safely sing that pitch? Higher notes, accented notes, sustained notes and louder notes, require more breath.

Working with singers in musicals where there is dancing choreography is a perfect place to start planning the breath. Starting with the National Company of *"A Chorus Line"* in 1980, I have had the privilege of working with professional dancers who have to sing and dance at the same time.

When performers come in for a lesson with injuries to the vocal cords, I have to figure out a way they can stay in the show and get rid of the nodes or just improve the function of the cords. I would have them show me the moves of the dance while singing the song and see where they are not sending enough breath through the throat for the pitches. Dancers hold their stomachs in to support their backs and this is the first place to look for the problem and the correction.

Take any song, look at the music and see where the notes go up on the staff. Those points need more breath, a buttocks squeeze, a tummy move will give you that support on that note. Then look at the words and the movement of the tongue. Use the tongue quickly in forming the word and move that sound with the breath over the tongue and out the lips.

For singer/dancers in Musicals I go through each song and plan where to send up more breath with the choreography of the dance. Practice breathing the song, not singing, just breathing the song. Do it lying down and relaxing. Think and plan the breaths at the higher, louder, accented and sustained notes. Plan where to bring the tummy in and when to squeeze the buttocks. Then do the dance and the breathing for the song, not singing, just using the breath with the movement needed for the song. Do this for a couple of the songs it will become more natural and easier with each song.

For random moves while singing with a band, practice sending up enough breath in each pitch with the movement. I strongly suggest that you develop a lot of endurance in singing by exercising physically while singing. You will get the stamina to sing safely. Singers who are physically active while performing, need to get in good physical shape. The whole body is necessary with healthy singing.

When playing guitar or bass, practice breathing with your instrument at the abdomen to feel the tummy movement against the instrument. It is important to make that connection.

I used to play guitar and sing at the same time and often forgot to breathe. I was too busy playing. Take a song, play the instrument and practice the breathing in the song but don't sing it. Then make a track. Record yourself playing the song. Hold the instrument but don't play, sing the song with the breathing. Then put it all together. Once you have wood-shedded a couple of songs it will become easier. I also suggest at first to just play chords and not all the intricate moves until the breath is coordinated.

Student Feedback

*"I cannot begin to tell you how much Suzanne's technique has saved my singing career. She came into my life when I starred in the Broadway hit **"Fosse"** where I had to do intense singing while dancing simultaneously. We worked on choreographing my*

breathing, a technique I had never done with previous coaches. This allowed me to perform eight times a week with great strength and not over-extend my voice (which I was doing prior to working with Suzanne). Not only is Suzanne an amazing vocal coach, she is also what I call a vocal doctor! Her knowledge of the vocal anatomy is immense. This knowledge has allowed me to sing through any type of illness that affects my voice. From nasty colds and flus to even a total loss of my speaking voice.

I had a show in Palm Springs one year where I had lost my speaking voice due to allergies. In association with my ENT and Suzanne's magic I was able to sing that night. I thank God my dear friend Jacquey Maltby introduced me to this incredible woman who is not only my Vocal Guru but also a dear friend."

Valarie Pettiford

Valarie Pettiford is a supreme Bob Fosse Dancer, wonderful singer and actress, nominated for a Tony for the Broadway Musical, ***"Fosse." "Fosse"*** dancers are very stylized often with angular poses. Dancers hold in the abdominals to support their backs and to give that centered strength. This will lead to no support for singing. After I had worked to choreograph the breath for every number Valarie did, she went off to Broadway. One night while Ms Pettiford was performing in ***"Fosse,"*** she called me in a panic. She said "I'm on in five minutes and my voice isn't working." I had her sing a few exercises and said "your voice is fine; you just aren't breathing." I heard someone say "Ms Pettiford you're on." Off she went and not until I saw her back in Los Angeles a month later, did I ask her how she had done. She said, "I sang like a songbird."

Chapter 6
The Mighty Tongue and Breathing

The tongue is a key to singing and speaking, as each word must be formed by this very mobile muscle. Each consonant requires a slightly different shape of the tongue to form that sound. Say "forming the words" in slow motion and feel how busy the tongue is, rising and falling like a wave.

 If you were a referee of the voice you would call interference on the tongue all the time as it can be the root of many vocal problems. It is a large and powerful muscle connected to the larynx. If the back of the tongue is tight, so is the larynx as it is attached to the back of the tongue. The tongue and the larynx need to be in a relaxed state when speaking or singing. Activating the tongue should take place only at the middle and front of the tongue, near the lips. Then there is no interference with the breath at the back of the throat.

To feel your tongue, place your thumb and fingers underneath your jaw, at the bend where the head meets the neck. Move the tip of the tongue to the roof of the mouth. You will feel the back of the tongue fall into your fingers.

Problem:
Singers and speakers tend to form words with the back of the tongue, muscling to form the word and the sound. This is very stressful for the tongue, larynx, and vocal folds.

Solution:
Form the words with the front of the tongue and lips, with the breath carrying the voice through the lips and out the mouth. When you articulate words with the front of the tongue and the lips, using your breath at the same time, stress is removed from the throat. The timing, coordination of the breath, and use of the tongue and lips will determine the freedom of vocal production.

Problem:
Anytime vocal improvisation is used, as in country music, rhythm and blues, and jazz, singers tend to feel they need to use the back of the tongue to achieve a specific sound. This tightens the larynx and displaces the vocal folds, leading to abuse of the voice.

Solution:
It is possible to change the placement of words to the front of the mouth and maintain the sound. As in everything with singing, let the energy of the breath take care of the movement of the improvisations, the changing of the pitches. Think about using the lips more for word generation. Lips are not just for kissing. They help tremendously in the articulation of words and in moving the tone forward in and out of the mouth.

Problem:
Some singers make too much space in the back of the throat by pushing down the back of the tongue. Space is not necessarily a bad thing. Singers lift the soft palate, in the back of the throat, to execute high notes. But, pressing down the back of the tongue pushes the larynx down and is the root of many vocal problems. I have found some classically trained singers depress

the back of the tongue to make space which produces what I call "a swallowed sound." This in turn causes tension on the vocal structures.

Solution:
Pressing the tongue down in the back can feel like opening the throat. However, the throat is open when we are relaxed. It's important to know that when the back of the tongue is relaxed there is enough space for sound generation.

Problem:
Singers hold the sound in the throat once they've hit a note in an effort to control the sound. If a player does this with a wind instrument, the sound stops. The voice can be forced out in spite of the blockage, but this takes its toll on the structures, putting tension on the vocal folds.

Solution:
Singers must learn how to let the voice be free. The breath should supply the energy and the vocal power, not the muscles of the throat.

Problem:
Pitch problems are caused by the lack of breath and tension on the back of the tongue. If the pitch is flat, the back of the tongue is depressed and there is not enough air. If the pitch is sharp, the tongue is being forced up in "reaching" for the note without enough breath.

Solution:
Relax the back of the tongue to allow the breath to carry the sound to the front of the mouth and out the

lips. Form the words with the front of the tongue and the lips.

WORDS:
Words require the Mighty Tongue, the lips and enough breath to carry them out the mouth. The problem with words is in the timing of the movement of the tongue in forming the words.

Consonants: B, D, F, M, N, P, S, T, V, and Z can help move the sound out the lips because they are formed more forward in the mouth. The C, K sounds or G, J, L Q all have lots of tongue action and the timing of moving the tongue quickly to resting position after the forming of those consonants is very important to freeing your voice. Keep the sound moving forward with the tongue quickly out of the way. Hit and drop, which means to quickly drop the tongue after forming the word.

Take words like *Love, Lift, Like,* and *You*, and stop mid-word to feel where the tongue is, then drop it quickly with the tip of the tongue touching the back of your bottom teeth. It is good to try these things slowly, so you have a true sense of how the tongue works.

Vowels: the E sound can easily spread the tongue and block the sound. I have found that pronouncing the E more like IH, silent H, puts the tongue in more open "in oral space" so the tone can more easily travel out the lips. For instance: Green (Grihn) or Dream (Drihm). Try it and see how the opening in the mouth changes yet it still sounds like an E.

Try This:

1. Put the tip of the tongue at the back of the bottom teeth. Relax the tongue. Just let it sit there in the bottom of the mouth like it weighs many pounds. Don't push it down. Just let it sit. Send sound over the tongue, sustaining a note with the support of the breath, aiming the sound to the roof of the mouth.

2. Connect words together, like "I'lltellthemaninthestreet". This takes the work away from the throat and puts the words at the front of the tongue. This technique can be used with legato and staccato lines.

3. The trumpet connection. Using the tongue as a singer is much like using it for tonguing a trumpet. Use the sound "ta". The forward and smallest part of the tongue is used to articulate the sound, just behind the top teeth, and when done, falls immediately back down behind the lower teeth. Repeating syllables of "ta" is a good exercise for the tongue. On each syllable, the tongue "hits and drops". On each hit and drop, the tongue moves between the upper teeth and the lower teeth (single tonguing).

Next, move to more advanced tongue exercises, like those a trumpet player uses. "Tu ku, tu ku, tu ku" (double tonguing) and "tukuto, tukuto" (triple tonguing). The K consonant is harder, as many singers form it with the back of the tongue, and if it isn't relaxed quickly, it can easily block the movement of the breath.

4. Sticking the tongue straight out "un-kinks" it. Move the tongue to the left and to the right, then up to the nose. This is a good way to take stress out of the tongue, especially the back area.

5. Imagine trying to keep a feather in the air with your breath. The breath energy needed to keep the feather in the air must be present when you're speaking or singing.

Background Research:

I am a person who wants to understand how the voice works. Any person who has something to add to what I already know is worthy of investigation. Quite a few years ago, my research of TMJ or Temporomandibular Joint and Muscle Disorder, brought me to Oral Myologist, Barbara Greene. I spent hours with her showing me pictures of children with faces with features askew. Jaws were crooked, teeth were crooked, and eyes weren't in a normal position on the face. She showed me exercises for the tongue that within six months or so, corrected the children's faces so they looked normal. This to me was a whole different way of looking at the power of the tongue and the conditions that can affect the oral structure.

I look at mouths all day when teaching. I see lots of action with the movement of the tongue. I see how the tongue affects pitch and how easily it interferes with the production of sound. I see how it is directly linked to vocal injuries.

The back of the tongue is connected by the hyoid bone to the larynx so any tension there will affect the freedom of the voice.

Barbara Greene showed me the effects of the tongue on one's bite and the position of the teeth. The tongue can affect the shape of the oral cavity, the jaw and the roof of the mouth.

The inner part of the mouth, the oral cavity, is the channel for the sound. Alignment of the structures, properly supported by the breath to carry the sound is the goal for speaking and singing.

Ms. Greene's demonstrations of tongue exercises helped me to understand more clearly the musculature's involvement in forming the words.

If you wish more information on Oral Myology Therapy, Barbara Greene's website is: **www.tonguethrust.com**

Remember:

- Relax the back of the tongue.

- Use the lips.

- Make sure there is enough breath to send over the tongue for every pitch and word.

Chapter 7
Mouth/Palate/Jaw and Breathing

Each of us has a different shaped mouth both inside and out. It is our acoustical center and it is important to understand its function in singing.

The roof of the mouth is where we send the sound to vibrate and resonate, and where the vibrato will be. Look in the mirror. Open your mouth and look at the roof of the mouth. What shape is it? Look at the channel or raised area for the breath to hold the vibration.

"Singing forward" is placing the vibration in the front of the mouth, behind the top teeth for focus and direction. The voice needs to be carried by the breath through the throat, over the back of the tongue, to the roof of the mouth, and then through the lips.

Picture the roof of the mouth like the dome of a cathedral. A listener in a cathedral can hear the vibrations of sound go back and forth, bouncing off the sides and the top, resonating. This is how the singer shapes the sound in the mouth.

Problem:
If the soft palate isn't raised, the space is diminished. For higher notes it is difficult to accurately hit the notes from the right place, on top of the note.

Solution:
"Making space" is important to understand because misinterpretation can be hazardous to vocal health. When singing, the soft palate rises to make space, but shouldn't spread wide as this causes tension on the vocal folds. The soft palate is like a curtain that needs

to be raised so the sound has no resistance and can freely move through the mouth.

Problem:
Pitch: flat or sharp. Inconsistent pitch is due to incorrect singing, not enough breath for the given pitch and tension on the back of the tongue. If the singer has a good musical ear the temptation to micro-correct the pitch also causes vocal tension.

Solution:
Relax the back of the tongue, send up enough breath for the pitch and form the words with the front of the tongue and the lips. A singer can visualize the approach to a given pitch. Lifting, raising, sound energy, moving forward and getting on top of the note are all helpful phrases used to get the breath moving correctly in the "cathedral" - the roof of the mouth.

Problem:
Not enough breath.

Solution:
The movement of the sound must be supported and carried by the breath traveling forward from the back of the neck, up and over, vibrating at the roof of the mouth and out the lips. For the sound to travel it must have the energy of the breath to carry it.

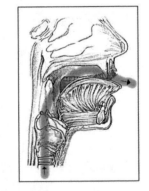

Problem:
Tightness in the jaw creates resistance to the free movement of sound out of the mouth.

Solution:

The jaw needs to relax so as to not interfere with the

movement of sound. Place your fingers on each side of the face, between the cheek bones and lower jaw or use the heals of your hands as shown in the illustration.

The mouth should drop open, no forcing, just letting go. Our chewing muscles can put lots of stress on the jaw and cause what I call the "chomping effect" on the production of sound.

When you see a shaking jaw mostly with contemporary rhythm and blues singers it is stress on the jaw with tension on the back of the tongue and larynx that causes the shaking. Of course this action is very hazardous to the vocal folds, causing great stress.

Try This:

1. Make sounds with relaxation of the face, jaw, and palate. A yawn activates the soft palate. A sigh raises the palate for a higher sound. No force is necessary as the breath takes care of the structures.

2. Hum, placing your hands on the face to feel the vibrations, cupping the hands over the nose, lips, and chin.

3. Bend over, dropping the head down so the air falls over from the back of the neck. The breath carries the vibration across the roof of the mouth. When you're

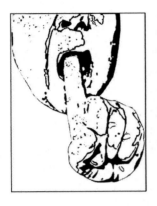

upside-down, it can be easier to feel a relaxed throat, allowing for the breath to come from the back of the neck, up and over the roof of the mouth.

4. Put a finger in the mouth, pressing against the hard palette where it curves behind your top teeth. Now sing an ascending scale sending the vibration of sound up your finger, using the finger as a sounding board. The top side of the finger should face the inside of the mouth. You should feel the highest note at the fingernail, the lowest at your knuckle.

5. Use the weight of the heel of the hands on the side of the face to relax the jaw, making the mouth an oval. Remove the hands and look in the mirror for the shape of the roof of the mouth. Then make your lips into that shape. This shape focuses your particular sound. It is the most focused placement area in your oral cavity.

Chapter 8
The Larynx and Breathing

The one voice teacher I had taught opera exclusively: Bel Canto, Garcia-Marchesi Method. I was interested in working on musical theatre pieces, jazz, blues and folk music. This teacher had no interest in anything but opera, which is not uncommon with traditional vocal instructors. As with piano or any other instrument one studies, classical music is the basis of serious study of your voice.

I had decided that if I were ever to teach voice, I would teach all uses of the voice. In my opinion any method is worthless unless it is taught by someone who truly understands how the vocal instrument works.

I have had students, over the years, who have studied all over the world: in Universities, Colleges, Music Conservatories and with local voice teachers. They often have heard similar things about vocal production that I say and teach. But I consistently find these teachers don't understand the larynx. Voice students have learned to lower the larynx, or put it in various positions for different effects. They have been taught to spread out the back of the throat or lower the back of the tongue to make space. They have been taught all kinds of moves which involve the larynx but still tell me they were taught to relax the larynx.

In order to repair a voice I teach the student not to lower the larynx or spread out the back of the throat or move the larynx in any way but to let it SIT THERE just like it does when you are doing nothing. Only then can I fix the voice and develop it to be free enough to sing any music you wish to sing or speak or scream, without harm.

The vocal mechanism can be seen and videotaped with endoscopy. In this procedure, a doctor puts a small tube to view the larynx from the nose or mouth. The person speaks or sings and the structures are viewed.

Working with Dr. Schneider, I have viewed this procedure. What I saw when the singer pushed the larynx down was the cricoid cartilage moving and blocking the view of the vocal folds. The blockage encouraged the singer to force the notes.

The vocal equipment we naturally feel is in the front of the throat. This presents a problem, because we want to control the voice there. The breath comes through the larynx, but think about it coming from the spine in order to have the breath approach the vocal folds from the correct position so the folds aren't stretched, forced, or manipulated to form the tone or pitch.

 ● Place your hand on the front of the throat, thumb on one side and fingers on the other. You will feel a hard, cartilaginous structure. This is the larynx. Gently wiggle it back and forth. It should move a little bit in both directions. This is what a relaxed larynx feels like, and how yours should feel when you're speaking or singing.

The wonderful larynx can be your best friend if you treat it well. It needs to be fed with breath. Without feeding, it tightens and the battle begins. When the larynx wins, you lose. It needs to be fed with breath, and then left alone. When asked to do something it's not designed to do, it will rebel and interfere with the function of the vocal folds, which in turn lose their elasticity and brilliance. If the folds are abused over time, they become injured. Trust the breath and feed the larynx with breath and the vocal folds will be free to make beautiful sounds.

Problem:
Singers sometimes lower the larynx to achieve a deeper or more powerful sound. Lowering the larynx is often taught to students. Opera singers, especially, want a huge space to make a huge sound, so they lower the larynx. This in turn brings the vocal folds down, and they develop tension.

Solution:
Why would a singer want to bring the structures down when the breath must move up and out the mouth? It is not necessary to lower the larynx for any reason, or to produce any type of sound. It is vital to keep the larynx relaxed at all times for vocal health.

Problem:
The larynx is lowered out of habit on inspiration of the breath, or when using the larynx to help "draw in" the breath.

Solution:
Practice taking a silent breath, using the diaphragm without using the larynx to draw in the breath and learn to incorporate this into singing. For singing and speaking a relaxed larynx is the key.

Problem:
Lack of breath, improper placement of words, tongue interference, and jaw tension all cause tension on the larynx.

Solution:

Being a detective is important to both teacher and student. Learn to palpate the larynx and assess it for tightness to assess and treat the root of the problem. Feel the larynx with three fingers on each side when you are not singing or speaking, you should be able to move it gently from side to side. When you sing or speak do the same thing. The only thing you should feel is vibrations moving not the structures.

Problem:

Throat infection and acid reflux are conditions causing swelling and affecting the mobility of the larynx, making it difficult to sing. The natural response is to force the sound through. This can cause injury.

Solution:

See a physician to take care of infection and acid reflux. Exercise your voice. Narrowly place the vibrations behind your face, an imaginary line from the middle of your chin to the bridge of your nose. Avoid tension of the larynx and use enough breath throughout the exercise. Humming is a good way to focus the voice and carry it out your mouth. Feel the vibration on your lips, chin, and cheeks. Exercise circulates the blood for a natural healing.

Problem:

Inflammation. Singers say "My technique is fine but I got sick and couldn't get back on track." It's easy to get sloppy, but if you rely on your voice it is imperative to keep it in good working order with a healthy technique.

Solution:

No tension on the larynx and place the voice properly forward in the mouth with enough breath to carry the sound out your lips. If you are sick, warm up slowly and be very focused in the placement of the voice. It will take longer than usual to warm up.
Circulation, movement in the vocal tracts, promotes healing.

Problem:

We learn to vocally edit, stopping the natural flow of speaking to be careful about what we say. This tightens the larynx.

Solution:

We have muscle memory and automatic responses in almost every function of our busy lives. The way we speak is built in and automatic and thus it is easy to speak in a vocally harmful way. Repetition of proper technique goes a long way toward breaking bad habits and developing good vocal habits.

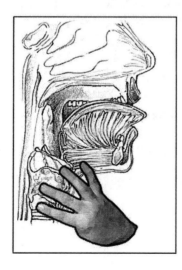

Try This:

Place your three center fingers on the larynx. Sing a phrase or two and feel if there is tension or a shifting of the larynx (vibration is fine). It should be relaxed even when you are singing. Does it move on specific notes or words? If so, try expelling more air at those points. This should help relax the larynx.

Case Study One:
John Rubinstein was starring in *"Ragtime"* in Los
Angeles at the Schubert Theatre. He played a very
vocally challenging part, requiring movement in the
staged songs. He came to me as a last resort to repair
nodes he'd developed on his cords. He had been on
three weeks vocal rest by his doctor, but the nodes
were still there and he was in danger of losing his part.
Mr. Rubinstein had been taught many years before,
while on Broadway, how to lower the larynx. I taught
him to use the breath without moving the larynx. In one
lesson he was able to produce enough change to
continue the show. As Mr. Rubinstein states in the
introduction, his voice got richer and stronger than it
had ever been.

Case Study Two:
I was asked to help a TV actress sing on a special. I
met her for the first time the night before she had to
sing. She had a cold and was vocally very thick, throat
puffy and swollen. She had been speaking all day,
while filming the show, and was tired. I taught her the
basic principles of breathing and a relaxed larynx. She
had two songs to do, so I had her warm up slowly and
then we worked on the songs.

The next day, after filming the TV show once again, we
went to the recording studio to record with the
orchestra. There was a four hour wait, so she warmed
up periodically so as not to cause fatigue. Each time it
became easier and quicker to keep the circulation
flowing. By the time she recorded, she was fine.

Chapter 9
The Larynx and Boys' Vocal Change

The larynx doubles in size when boys go through puberty and it happens pretty quickly. If the young man has been singing happily as a soprano it is disconcerting to all of a sudden 'not have control' of his voice.

I was working with Chris, a boy soprano, who was having a lot of success singing for movies and TV. When he first got a job working on the movie *UNDER THE TUSCAN SUN*, he was a soprano. He was to sing for the wedding scene off camera. It was a lovely chant in Latin. His performance was successfully completed but later the composer wanted to change a few things.

When Chris was called back to re-record, he was starting to go through the vocal change. I worked with him to keep that soprano going, and Chris being a smart and talented musician, was able to do it beautifully.

When the larynx is free, the change is much easier. If the boy has used and manipulated the larynx to make his higher notes, then it will be much more difficult to learn to sing with a larger, adult sized larynx. If he learns to sing with a relaxed larynx, the transition will go faster and be a lifelong change for a freely singing voice.

The freedom in the singing is more important than making impressive vocal sounds by spreading the larynx, dropping it and pressing down the back of the tongue. I have found the problem more with males than females, especially those with classical or traditional training.

I have had many men come in for lessons whose voices sound big and impressive to the average ear, but when I touch the larynx, I detect great tension. Your ears can deceive you and it feels powerful to hear this big voice coming out of your mouth. After all of these years teaching I usually can hear the strain, a swallowed sound, tension on the tongue and larynx being the culprit.

Recently, I had four young male students going through the stress of vocal change. One of them had a huge range but the sound was produced with a lot of laryngeal manipulation. This means the larynx was moving all over the place. He was a Celine Dion fan and he imitated all her vocal moves – putting great stress on the larynx. He also imitated Mariah Carey with all the rhythm and blues maneuvers – again with vocal stress by moving the larynx to produce the vocal improvisations.

I told him, he should no longer move the larynx, but rather use his breath to move those sounds. He was resistant because that is how he learned to imitate these talented singers. He told me he felt sore after singing like that and all of a sudden his voice wouldn't work. The shaking jaws, tight tongues and forced singing are all visible when contemporary rhythm and blues voices are imitated by young singers.

With the change, a young man's voice drops about an octave and they lose tone in the middle register. It is very confusing to them and they struggle in the larynx trying to find how and where to place their voice. Once they experience letting go of the larynx and learn to use their breath effectively, the problem no longer exists.

Chapter 10
The Vocal Folds and Breathing

The vocal folds are suspended in animation. The breath keeps them afloat. The vocal folds eagerly await the movement of breath to carry vibration forward into the mouth.

Picture a hang glider jumping off a cliff and catching the air current to keep afloat, riding the air. Tipping the wings of  the hang glider can cause movement out of the air current. The vocal folds need the air current, or breath, to keep vibrating. We supply the breath with our abdominal muscles to keep the cords vibrating without tension, allowing full range in the voice and power and versatility for different styles of music.

Problem:
Without the breath they go to a resting position, and if the person is still speaking or singing they will have tension on the folds, the larynx, and the tongue.

Solution:
To keep the folds suspended, send up enough breath, relax the tongue and larynx, and form words at the front of the tongue and lips. Think of the torso like a tube of toothpaste. Squeeze from the bottom and let the breath fly out the top.

Problem:

When the back of the tongue is used in forming words, it will interfere with the movement of the breath and the breath carrying the sound falls back into the throat.

Solution:

Relax the tongue quickly and send the breath over the tongue and out the lips. The breath must be continuously moving forward throughout each phrase

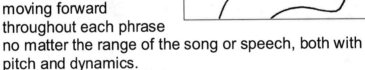

UP...OVER...OUT

no matter the range of the song or speech, both with pitch and dynamics.

Problem:

Singers tend to use tension in the vocal folds because there is a feeling that something isn't right in the throat, so they try to force the sound out.

Solution:

Relax and send the breath through. A good kick of breath from the abdomen will release tension in the throat.

Remember:

- Love your larynx and let it be!

- A relaxed larynx and vocal cords are the key.

- Trust the air currents, or the breath.

Chapter 11
Torso Muscles and Breathing

A singer needs to take excellent care of the vocal instrument. Align the body to give the best possible support for the use of breath. The torso should be erect but not tense. This allows the abdominals and lower back muscles to function.

Learning how to use the abdominal muscles with the movement of breath is probably the most important lesson in healthy singing. The abdominals should be flexible, not rigid. Without the abdominals, using the voice would be like driving a car without gas. The breath is the energy that "sparks" the vocal folds, getting them to vibrate. The breath also carries the sound forward in the mouth and out the lips.

As we inhale, the abdominals need to expand as the diaphragm moves down, filling the lungs with air. As we exhale, the abdominals contract, propelling the air out of the lungs, through the throat and out the lips.

Try This:
1. Stand against a wall and press the shoulders back, making them touch the wall. This is an upright posture.
2. Exercise the back, arms, and shoulders to develop support for the breathing mechanism.
3. While standing, place your hands over the bellybutton. This is the center of the abdominal muscles. Press in quickly, as if someone just punched you in the belly. A whosh of air will come out your mouth. There

are variations in the movement of the abdominals, and it is important to experiment with your own muscles to see what pressure you need on a given pitch and in changing volume and pitch.

4. Place both hands on your chest, crisscrossed above the breasts. First, breathe into the chest, raising it up. Then exhale and let the chest fall, heaving a sigh. Do this three times to relax the chest. Now try inhaling by expanding below the bottom of the bra line, diaphragm, central and lower abdominals. Let the chest relax. It's good to put the weight of the hands on the chest because you will feel if you are raising the chest or relaxing it. The hands on the chest can also sense the expansion of the diaphragm and the movement of the abdominals.

The BRA LINE is the circumference of the body just under the breast.

5. Practice loosening the neck. Drop the head gently forward, then look up to the ceiling. Move the head slowly side to side. Raise the shoulders up to the ears, hold, and release. Do this several times to loosen the shoulders.

6. Practice using the abdominals to produce sound. With the body at rest, take a full, silent breath. Hiss softly, letting a small amount of air through the lips as you slowly contract the abdominals. Now take another quiet breath, and pulse the hiss, contracting the abdominals each time.

7. The abdominals are important to sing higher, to sing louder, to sustain notes, and to accent a note. Each of these requires varying degrees of abdominal pressure. Practice each of these techniques with a hand on the abdomen to monitor your movement.

Case Study:

I worked with a dancer from *"A Chorus Line"* who had breath support problems. I think of dancers as athletes, and thus in good physical shape. Dr. Schneider said, "Her back is probably weak. In fact, this is a problem for most singers." I had never thought about how a weak back would affect breath production. Now I recognize the important role of physical support, posture, and strength.

My experience in working with the National Tour of *"A Chorus Line"* when they were in Los Angeles, had a huge impact on me realizing the importance of choreographing the breath. One of the performers said she had trouble in a number where she was dancing and had to sing quick lines. I went through the number with her dancing in my studio and told her when she needed to time her abdominal movement with her dance moves - on which word she needed more air. Her problems ended with that song and she was able to carry the action into her big solo numbers.

When dancers study ballet, they are taught to lift at the sternum, hold their tummies in, and tighten their abs and chest. While this is good posture for dancing it can be hazardous for singing.

Dancing requires so much strength and practice if one chooses to be a professional. To last, dancers must stay in good shape. I have always had great respect for the dancers' commitment.

When I was preparing Christina Applegate for her first Broadway show, *"Sweet Charity"*, she would come to her singing lessons having danced for 5 hours. As tired as she was she never missed a second of work singing and learning the songs. She had that professional work ethic and she was determined to do her very best to be prepared. In this kind of work with students a teacher is developing the voice, and the singer defines the character with the voice. These components must work together. *"Sweet Charity"* is a dancing show and Christina is a terrific dancer and actress with little singing experience. What was magical for me was how she integrated it all. On opening night she came out with such confidence and the crowd fell in love with her. She had done the work and she was ready.

Never underestimate the value of the work.

Teaching in Los Angeles requires a certain mind set. Most often work has to be done very fast especially the repairing of the voice. In the middle of a recording or a show, the show must go on and so must the singer. I have to work fast to assess the damage and the immediate correction to solve the singer's vocal problems.

I learn so much from each situation and each student: the fears, the demands on the voice in these environs - the dryness of the atmosphere, the effects of food and drink, the directions in the performance given by someone who doesn't understand the voice (thereby confusing the singer and prompting vocal manipulation).

Oftentimes the director of a musical was a dancer and looks to the importance of movement more than the vocal performance. This puts great stress on the singer trying to accommodate the director's requirements. This is why it is so important to take great care of your body and your vocal instrument.

Singing with a band, especially rock music or any music where there is a lot of volume of sound can stress the voice. With electronic instruments the player can dial up the volume. From my experience with singers, that is what they are up against. The most important pieces of equipment you need as a singer are a monitor and a good microphone. You must learn how to use or play them like instruments. The microphone is an extension of the voice. It is a direct connection to your heart and soul and the voice that communicates to the audience. If you can't hear yourself singing, you will force and injure your voice. There are also ear monitors that some of my students have used successfully. Ear plugs are important to preserve your hearing. In my experience they block out the noise and amplification made by electronic instruments; but you can still hear yourself.

If I go to a rock rehearsal, I wear ear plugs. Remember your ears and vocal folds are irreplaceable; take care of them. No one else cares about your vocal equipment the way you must. Fight for your rights as a singer in a band. The guitar players can replace the guitar strings; the drummer can replace the drum heads. Protect yourself by being prepared and making sure monitors are there for rehearsals and performances. That can be your investment to preserve your vocal health and your precious ears.

"Suzanne Kiechle is a maverick in the field of vocal coaching. I have never met a voice teacher who can teach students to sing correctly while maintaining a sense of stylistic integrity. She is a master. I have worked with her for ten years and I have time and time again seen her fix vocal problems in a matter of minutes that would take others weeks, months, or years. The difference is her technique. She is truly a voice to be listened to because she knows what she is talking about.

Every singer should read her book."

Zooey Deschanel – Actress and Singer

Chapter 12
Vocally Preparing For Roles
For Singers and Actors

My vocal technique is valuable to singers and actors because it fits all types of music and all uses of the voice. All that's required is a relaxed larynx; enough breath for each pitch; and words formed in the front of the mouth.

● Janis Joplin, a blues, rock, singing, screaming, artist has been the center of several movies that have yet to be made. I had the good fortune of working with Zooey Deschanel on one such project. We worked for several months getting the gritty sounds and vocal power notes with the rockin' bluesy music of Janis Joplin.

Janis Joplin was a great project to validate my approach to singing healthy no matter the type of music. Zooey did a lot of research: talking to people who knew Janis, watching videos and listening to records of Janis singing in live concert. Ms. Deschanel then came to me to learn how to make those sounds without hurting her voice. We listened to Janis Joplin CD's and discussed the different sounds that Janis made. A song like **Ball and Chain**, has several very different kinds of sounds: deep bluesy full voice low notes, screams, and vocal sound effects.

I too did my homework imitating the sounds I heard and watching the energy Janis displayed while performing these songs. When you sing correctly, with no tension in the larynx and enough breath for every sound you make while placing the voice properly, you can sing hard rock music without hurting yourself.

I suggested that Zooey should workout physically while singing to build up the stamina necessary for playing Janis. It was exciting to hear Zooey singing just like Janis, with all the energy and gritty vocals and then turn around and sing with her own style which is totally clear. There was absolutely no damage – the work she did made her own voice stronger.

• I was called in to work with two actresses, Ellen Barkin and Veronica Cartwright, who were to play classical singers for the movie *MAN TROUBLE* (also starring Jack Nicholson). Neither actress was a singer but they learned to sing a Bach fugue and the Et Resurrexit, from The Bach B Minor Mass. The first being in German and the Mass in Latin.

I had about 15 hours to work with each actress. In order for these actresses to look authentic they had to physically sing using their whole bodies with the energy and precision of classical singers.

The opening number of the movie was a rehearsal scene and that is where they sang the fugue. They actually could sing the whole thing but in movies they often edit so you only see a part of it.

The director was very thrilled with their performance as was I. Musically they had to be right on with the actual singers.

In the final scene of the movie, they performed the Bach B Minor with a full orchestra and chorus and Ellen and Veronica came through with flying colors.

Actors study the body movements and the way singers carry themselves. They had to learn the music, not just the languages, but the beats, so they could coordinate the fugue.

I have great respect for actors who have to learn everything so fast for movies and television. The choir was made up of some of my students, my sisters, friends and some people from the local choirs. They all had to learn authentic singing of the Bach B Minor. It was exciting for all of us.

- I got a call from Emily Deschanel to work with her for an episode of *BONES*. She was asked to sing **Girls Just Want To Have Fun** for a scene in a karaoke bar. Emily didn't have much time to get ready to sing and she had to rehearse and film other scenes on the same day. We had a little time a few days before and some quick rehearsals at the studio on the day of the filming. We warmed up her voice and got the connection of the voice and her character in the song with just a piano track. She made only two takes and the second one was a keeper. No pre-records or after recording, just on the spot singing in the scene with all characters of the show in the audience. Emily did a great job and then went on to do more scenes.

"When I was asked to sing on my TV show BONES, I had to learn a song quickly. I hadn't sung in years, but in a couple of days Suzanne helped me get my voice to a place I was comfortable with. It required that I sing as my character. Suzanne completely understood that and helped me find my character's voice organically." **Emily Deschanel**

"Suzanne's unique approach can repair the worst damage on a voice. She worked with me when I had nodules and helped me heal my voice completely. Suzanne has a special understanding of the voice and vocal cords, and she does everything with a sense of fun!"

Emily Deschanel – Actress "Bones"

Chapter 13
Psychology and Singing

Occasionally I teach a person who appears to understand what I'm teaching but still gets "stuck" when putting the knowledge into practice. Sometimes the person needs time to clear up bad habits. But it can be an emotionally charged problem, many times not recognized by the singer. Permission to make a mistake is very important in a lesson, and I stress this with students. We are working together to solve the problem.

Chest Chakra (Heart, or emotional center)

Problem:
A person who has been criticized by parents or siblings, or made fun of in school, often inhibits the natural free expression of the voice. Some sing anyway, but end up pushing the voice in defiance or because they want to be heard. Holding onto emotions can make the chest area tight, then when speaking or singing this translates to tension of the larynx, tongue, and jaw, impeding the flow of breath.

Solution:
For constriction of the chest, breathe into the chest and then release the breath so it drops back down. Do this several times to relax the chest muscles. Now do abdominal breathing, keeping the chest and shoulders relaxed.

Throat Chakra (Communication center)

Problem:
Our nature is to use our voices to be heard and understood. If, as children, we are told to be quiet when we want to share what we feel, we feel punished. With negative consequences we will hold onto our throats, holding back emotional outbursts. This tightens the throat, the voice becomes inhibited, and fear of reprisal causes one to grab the voice before it leaves the throat.

Solution:
Learn to let go, let it out, and express yourself. What you have to say and sing is of value. It is important to you to be able to use your voice to release your emotions, to empower you to express who you are and what you feel. It is your voice, it is unique to you and it is good.

Looking back in American history at a time we as a nation are not very proud of, a time of slavery, the people weren't free but their voices were. Listening to those spirituals, we hear the pain, hopes and loves of a people who had to be heard. The music from that terrible period in history is beyond inspiring.

A song that touched me deeply as a child was **Sometimes I Feel Like a Motherless Child**. When I was about ten years old, I sang that song. It came from such a deep place. When I picked up an old bugle at that age, with bullet holes in it, I played the Blues.

We are all connected through music and each culture has a personal contribution to make. It is in us to express our innermost feelings to free the spirit within our souls.

I have a friend, Bonnie Eichar, who is a Reiki Master. It is a Japanese form of healing, bringing good energy into all areas of the body. We hold on to so much in our lives and forget that our minds, bodies and souls need to be tuned up and freed from our own self editing along with the pressures of life. Bonnie taught me and several friends how to do Reiki. Every Friday night we got together, and she guided us through meditation. Then we practiced Reiki on each other. Those evenings I slept so well because I was able to release, let go, let that loving energy in and give it to others.

I realized the value of Reiki in teaching singing when an actress who hadn't sung in awhile was cast in a Broadway musical. She was frantic about it. When she first came in, I had her sit in a chair and I put on a CD of what I call "cosmic music", and proceeded to do a little Reiki on her to relax her and get her to breathe without anxiety. She quickly relaxed and then I was able to start her voice lesson.

I look at freeing the voice as a healing tool for one's life. We are magnificent creatures and the more we realize that, the more we will lead a cherished life for ourselves and others.

Teaching voice is so much about tuning into someone, finding what each person feels and understands about singing. Singing is a very vulnerable activity because the person is exposing themselves. It is also a most rewarding experience, mentally, physically, and emotionally.

This book is about removing the impediments from the vocal experience thus allowing the joy of expressing your true self.

"In my twenties, while in vocal distress, Suzanne's technique was able to steer me out of trouble in record time, unmask a clear soprano voice and solidify a strong belt in the process, and make me a lifelong disciple of her technique. She has provided me with a healthy four octave range that's enabled me to realize the dream and rigors of an eight show schedule on tour and on Broadway.

The great thing about Suzanne is she has never stopped learning as well, so even though I live in New York City now, I feel it's imperative to come back to Los Angeles several times a year to check in with my mentor. If not for Suzanne Kiechle, I would not be enjoying my 30th year in show business."

Pamela Dayton
"The Producers" Broadway/National Tour

Appendix One:

The Vocal Pyramid

Picture a pyramid. At the base are the muscles of the abdomen, the buttocks, and the low back. Then there is the diaphragm, powering the breath and maintaining breath support throughout. The diaphragm relies on the strong muscles of the base of the pyramid, and good posture. Next comes a relaxed chest and shoulder. Above that, a relaxed larynx, tongue, and jaw for placement of the breath for a given pitch. The top of the pyramid is the brain, responsible for the timing and coordination of word formation, and the movement of the breath over the tongue to the roof of the mouth and out the lips.

I love the voice and all its complexities, colors, sounds, and emotion. I have been fascinated by singers since I was a little girl, sitting enthralled by stage singers, in love with the voice and the singer. Today I feel pain when I hear most singers, because I hear the tension in the voice and want to free it. I know if they learn to sing 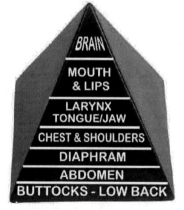 freely, they would become even better performers and I'd feel their freedom and joy.

It is popular these days to sound as though you're in pain. A forced, strained sound is fashionable. Too often musical theatre performers who have great voices begin to force and lose the quality they had upon arrival on Broadway. This obnoxious fashion is vocally destructive. There are safe ways to achieve power, emotion, and excitement. The voice is a precious instrument and if treated well can last a lifetime of pleasure.

A singer can be exciting and sing beautifully without strain. It is an athletic experience because singing with power and agility takes conditioning and practice. A singer needs to be in shape physically and vocally to be able to sing every night without injury. Be true to your own abilities and try not to sing like someone else with different vocal equipment, or who forces and strains their voice without thought for the future. Be smart about you and develop your instrument to be the best it can be. Yes, you can sing with all the emotion you want and not strain.

Appendix Two:

Checklist for Keeping the Voice Healthy

1. Hydration is a key. Drink water or Gatorade to stay hydrated. Avoid alcohol and coffee, which tend to dehydrate. Keep moisture in the vocal tract with steam or nasal spray. A humidifier or vaporizer in dressing room and bedroom keep moisture in the air. Ocean, nasal spray, or saline solution is great for hydration.

2. Bactroban salve, a prescription to put in the nose, helps keep the moisture in.

3. Carry a thermos of steaming water to take a whiff if conditions are dry. Don't let the nose touch the hot water, just breathe in the steam.

4. Use a vibrator to take tension away from the muscles of the shoulders and neck. I believe in the use of a good massage therapist, physical therapist, or chiropractor to help with the physical body.

5. Avoid acidic food and drink. Oily, spicy, creamy, or heavy foods are hard to digest. Find nourishing foods that don't affect the quality of your singing. Bananas can be a good fix. Protein is important to give the body strength. Those who suffer from acid reflux should not eat before bed. Discuss the use of acid reducing medication with your doctor.

6. Acid cough usually occurs in the morning. With a change of diet and not eating before bed, you can avoid this occurrence. If it does occur, I have found certain products helpful – but it is important to discuss the use of such acid controllers with your doctor.

*"Suzanne Kiechle's emergency
assistance was invaluable in allowing me
to complete the production of an album
on schedule. She substantially RESTORED
THE SINGER'S TIRED VOICE IN ONE
VISIT and enabled her (Chantal Kreviazuk) to
complete her Vocals on time."*

**Peter Asher – Senior Vice President,
Sony Records**

Appendix Three:

Suzanne's Guide for Successful Singing

1. Warm up the voice in the shower or in steam from the shower. Before rehearsals, performances, and before going to bed, do vocal exercises. The exercises I recommend before bed are simple and take only a few minutes. When you work your voice out in a performance, there is going to be some natural swelling, as blood rushes to the surface.

2. The few minutes of 5 note scales from the top down, starting with low notes, for women; on **Na** ,note, E above middle C down to A below middle C. Then E flat down to A flat etc. Humming in the lower register is also recommended. For Men; on **Na**, note G below middle C down to the C an octave from middle C. Anywhere in that region is a good place to start.

3. What I call "drip downs" in the higher register, falsetto for men and Soprano zone for the ladies both on the sound "E". All of these sounds should be placed forward in the mask. For high notes, lift the soft palate (top part of the yawn), and release the air placed from the top part of the soft palate and then go down 5 notes "eee oooo" making sure you use your buttocks to ease out those notes with your breath.

4. To locate the placement forward, put your 1st finger pressing at the hard palate behind your top teeth, with your finger nail facing the back of the throat. Keep the vibrations lifted to the roof of your mouth at all times. Do not let breath support drop.

5. After hard workouts, lie down and practice breathing, visualizing the choreography while relaxed. Review the steps and the breath necessary in songs: high notes, sustained notes, louder notes.

6. After resting, go through the choreography, breathing the song as you move, keeping the voice forward.

Appendix Four:

Sample Breathing Exercises

Find a comfortable spot to lie down and relax, with no distractions. Turn off the cell phone.

Concentrate on the breath coming in and going out. Place your hands on top of your chest. Take some breaths in the chest to relax the chest. Breathe in slowly and let the breath out. Do this three times, very slowly, then relax the chest and expand the diaphragm.

Get the abdominals in the act, moving with the breath. On inhalation the abdominals expand; on exhale, release the muscles and let the air fly out of your mouth. Purse your lips like you're blowing out a candle and blow breath through the lips.

Take a silent breath by opening your mouth like a hole and expanding the diaphragm and abdominals. The air will go into the lungs all by itself so you don't need to use the larynx or throat to draw in the breath.

Relax the chest and let the breathing take place below the bottom of the bra line.

Once you are relaxed and the breath is coming easy and free, do these exercises.

1. Drop the jaw, relax the tongue, take in a breath, then close your lips and let the breath go "puh" out the lips

2. Take another relaxed breath, keeping the abdomen extended and hiss slowly, letting a little air out at a time, hissing through the lips, slowly contracting the abdominals.

3. Hissing while moving the abdominals in and out, with varying degrees of air pressure, helps to change

the volume of sound and pitches. An active abdomen is
key to supporting breath.

Appendix Five:

Each of my students receives a personal exercise program as part of the lesson. Here is a sample of vocal exercises.

Sample Vocal Preparation Exercises

1. Breathe deeply three times slowly and fully into the chest, letting the air release on the exhale. This is to release tension.
2. Bend over, letting the arms dangle and the head drop to relax the neck and shoulders.
3. While bent over, hum through the lips, feeling the forward placement of sound. Sing "may, ah, oh, ooh" in that position, and "nah"s up the five note scale.
4. Relax the chest, breathing below the bra line with the diaphragm and abdominals. Expand with the inhale, contracting the abdominal muscles with the exhale.
5. Proceed with vocal warm-up exercises. Warm up a couple of hours before singing to loosen up and eliminate drainage. Do a warm-up just before performance to get the voice focused and the breath connected to the movement of sound.

*"In Suzanne Kiechle's vocal
students one encounters a rare combination
of confidence in the MECHANICS OF VOCAL
PRODUCTION along with a REFRESHING
SENSE OF FREEDOM IN THE SINGING."*

**Peter Matz – Record Producer, Aranger,
and Conductor**

Appendix Six:

Creative Problem Solving for Performers

Singers with Instruments:
Musicians who sing while playing an instrument may have a hard time singing correctly with effective support because of the microphone position. Often the neck is strained to reach the microphone, or the head twisted, cutting off the breath.

I strongly recommend a microphone attached to the head or lavaliere. When playing piano, position the instrument so the performer can see the audience without twisting the neck or body. Have a supportive chair while playing piano.

Using a Microphone:
Place the microphone in front of the mouth, like an ice-cream cone. For low notes, slightly bring back the head; for high notes, slightly drop the head so air pressure comes up and over from the spine area toward the lips.

Emotion:
Some singers feel they can't sing emotionally without force or strain. It is possible to make any vocal sound without injury using the theories taught in this book.

Ritual:
Most singers benefit from creating a ritual for themselves, both of practicing everyday and also before each performance. The singer's body is like an athlete's body and preparation helps. Good vocal

habits are something a singer can rely on and can become second nature. The ritual should contain elements of relaxation, visualization, stretching, and breathing. Give yourself enough time to do the ritual, without interruption. This is your sacred time.

Auditions:

Choose material to fit your voice. There should be no vocal struggle or pitch problems in the material. In other words, you can easily perform the song. Total connection on the song aids performance from beginning to end. Your concentration should never be distracted.

The use of a good subtext to the lyrics can help in bringing life to a song, and will keep you focused. Have different types of music in your repertoire, including ballads and up-tempo tunes depending on the part you want. If you find numbers that work for you, do them!

Performance:

Remember to warm up, as in your ritual. Give yourself time for meals, and do not eat a big meal or anything hard to digest just before the performance. Avoid fats, milk products, acidic foods, spicy food, and caffeine. Make sure you're hydrated.

Do not waste energy on the day of performance. Often nervousness gets a performer into frantic behavior on the day of performance, but learn to quiet yourself. Find a quiet and comfortable spot backstage or in your home. Plan time for relaxation and breathing before a performance.

Appendix Seven:

A Simple Guide for Warming Up the Choir

1. Physical stretches for the upper body
    a. Neck stretches, up, down, and to the sides. Do everything slowly and easily.
    b. Raise shoulders to the ears, and release. Roll ·shoulders back.
    c. Bend over from the waist, allowing the head to be in a relaxed position. Arms should hang like an ape.
2. Hum into the face, singing a low but comfortable pitch. Feel the vibrations in the front of the face, nose, chin, and lips. While sustaining the pitch, bring your body to an upright position, keeping the focus of the sound. When the body is upright, lift more breath to the face with pressure from the abdominals.
3. Relax the jaw. Take the heels of the hands to the face and gently push down the lower jaw so the mouth is open and oval. Singing a note in this position should produce a fuller and more focused tone.
4. Stick the tongue out and stretch it in all directions.
5. Incorporate breathing exercises.
    a. Practice inhaling silently, with an open mouth and diaphragm expanded.
    b. Use the abdominals to expel a breath on a syllable like "puh".
    c. Hiss softly, like a slow leak, concentrating on the abdominals.
    d. Use a vocal exercise to pair abdomen with producing and sustaining sound.
6. Lift the soft palate, as in a yawn.
7. Encourage singers to monitor the larynx, making sure it is relaxed when using the voice.

"It may seem an exaggeration to say that meeting Suzanne Kiechle changed my life, but she certainly changed the way I felt about myself and my performance. I came to Suzanne in an anxious state about an important cabaret I was doing. I had recently been working with another coach who had good information but I would leave the lessons depressed and with a sore throat. Walking into Suzanne's studio was a revelation. She immediately made the diagnosis of my particular problems and then gave me the tools to remedy them: simple, clear with no humbug. Her tremendous support and enthusiasm brought back my joy of singing, my confidence and enabled me to progress very quickly indeed. I couldn't believe it. Neither could anyone else when they heard me sing. Waiting nervously in the dressing room before the show, I phoned Suzanne. Would you warm me up? I asked. 'Sure,' she said, 'are you breathing?' In 3 minutes I was ready to go."

Giselle Wolf
London Cabaret Artist

Appendix Eight:

Along with private voice lessons, I offer a variety of classes for small groups. Here is a sampling of one such class, often taught in conjunction with an accomplished actor or actress. Please contact me for questions about upcoming classes and lessons.

Beginning Voice for Actors

12-15 weeks, 3 hour class each week. This class includes:

1. Vocal techniques for singing and speaking, with exercises to be taped by each student for practice.
- **a.** Basic but practical physiology of the voice and the mechanical part of vocal production.
- **b.** Exercises for breathing, vocal placement, and posture.
- **c.** Information on the correct use of the larynx.

2. Identify your vocal identity.
- **a.** To change or not to change.
- **b.** Building richness of tone and vocal versatility.

3. Presenting yourself on stage.
- **a.** Overcoming the fear of singing in front of people.
- **b.** How fear affects the voice in performance and auditions and how to correct it.

4. Learning to sing a song technically and for presentation on stage.

5. Final demonstration of all the elements of voice along with presentation in performance.

"Suzanne has the most UNCANNY ABILITY to repair, exercise, and stretch a vocalist WITHOUT CHANGING HIS OR HER STYLE. A true genius in her field, she has performed miracles for me and my clients."

Pete Anderson – Record Producer
(Sara Evans,
Dwight Yoakum,
Michelle Schocked)

Appendix Nine:

Vocal Injuries and How to Fix them

If someone comes to me with nodes or hemorrhaged vocal folds, I first show them how they probably got them. I give them a vocal technique lesson pointing out the changes they need to make in order to fix the problem. First they must know how it feels when the larynx is tight before they can correct the condition. I start with easy, narrowly focused tones, moving the vibrations of sound up and down the face. I start where the student seems to be the most comfortable. For some people it is low notes for others, high notes. I pinpoint the area of injury, where the vocal folds don't quite meet and vibrate freely allowing air to escape producing diminished tone.

Nodes are on specific pitches and in my experience, it usually means that the singer or speaker has not given enough breath to properly place that specific note in the song. This will cause stress on the vocal cord, and repetition will often cause injury. If it is a node and it is large, then more notes are compromised.

It is very important during the rehabilitation process that the singer does not overdo high notes or power notes because too much repetition can weaken the injured area. If there is a glitch, the immediate fear reaction is to hold in the throat to protect it. This panic response is the opposite of what you should do. The correct solution is to relax and allow the breath to go through the throat freely as it does in the sighing exercises. Start from the highest comfortable note and sign down in pitch, focusing the sound behind the front of your face. The areas of vocal focus are A: high notes – bridge of the nose or behind the top teeth; B: low notes - chin, lips; C: the mid-range notes - top teeth, lips.

Inconsistent breath control creates common problems such as:

- Hitting high notes within a phrase and then dropping breath support on descent.
- Poor forward placement of the lowest notes and words of the phrase.
- Lack of breath on the mid range notes.
- Dropping the breath back into the throat at the end of a phrase.

Solutions to these problem areas are found in:

- Lifting the soft palate.
- Sending up enough breath placed properly forward.
- Dropping the tongue immediately after the formation of the consonant.
- Opening the mouth for the vowel which sends the sound out through the lips.

Most people who come to me with nodes or hemorrhaged vocal folds got the vocal injury singing or speaking while sick with a bronchial condition and or a throat infection where there is a lot of throat irritation and congestion. The performer was doing a show, was tired but had to put on a performance. While it is possible to sing through some colds and infections you have to warm up longer and be so focused in your placement with plenty of breath to carry your voice throughout the performance. You must never take antihistamines when you have to speak or sing. Antihistamines dry the nose and in my experience get the congestion backed up into the pharanx area, (the back of the throat). You are actually more clogged and your vocal mechanisms are more compromised.

Colds often happen during rehearsal periods of shows due to long hours, close quarters with other people in dressing rooms, dancing, sweating and going into cold air.

Get plenty of rest, be vocally hygienic, don't drink out of other's cups, wash your hands, eat good healthy food, and take vitamins.

When you have vocal injury, don't push your voice. Gently exercise your vocal folds with very focused sounds going right into your face and out your lips. If you have to work the material for the show you are in, don't keep repeating the hard parts. It is better to think the words and placement and practice the breath. You will not tire so much that way. Do my drip down exercises with every note being focused in the front of the face and out through the lips.

If your vocal injuries are caused by incorrect singing or speaking because of undo and unnecessary stress on the vocal folds, the voice will heal while singing and speaking correctly. You must have correct placement of the voice forward into the mask and enough breath support at all times with no larynx tension and relaxation of the back of the tongue.

Case History:

When I first met Mr. C, he was in a show in Los Angeles, and he had nodes. He was working with another voice teacher at the time but the node was still there and so was the struggle to get the sound out. I worked with him very briefly before he was cast in a musical tour of a Broadway show. As far as I could tell, the nodes were gone and his vocal folds were clean with no vocal obstruction.

After months of touring Mr. C was diagnosed with hemorrhaged vocal folds, which are weakened blood vessels that bleed. His nodes had returned as well. He was in Philadelphia, the home of the International Voice Foundation, where the doctor was ready to operate in three or four days. Other doctors in other cities had also suggested they would operate but wanted to wait to see if the problem would abate. Basically Mr. C was looking at a grim prognosis. Up to $1800 for the first visit, surgery in 3 or 4 days, three months of vocal rehabilitation (putting Mr. C out of work for that period of time), then a year of no singing before he could resume his career.

Mr. C turned to me for remedial work before accepting the medical recommendations. He had a three week window before he had to either get back to work or face a year starting with surgery and continuing vocal rehabilitation. We worked for two half hour sessions a week at first then added a few hours for a total of seven hours of vocal exercises, over a period of three weeks to relieve the stress on his injured vocal folds. It was important to address the songs he had to sing in the show by placing the songs properly in his voice.

After the seven hours, Mr. C returned to the show, node gone, hemorrhaged vocal folds cleared up with a total cost of $800, paid for by Workman's Comp.

About a month later, Mr. C called me from Florida after being on the road with the same show. He said his cords were clear, no more hemorrhage or nodes, but he had an inflammation of the pharanx (Pharangitis). He wanted to know if he should go into the show that night or stay away for a few days. With his history, I felt he should rest and not take chances by performing for a couple of days until he was better. If I had been in Florida at the time, and it was essential for him to perform, I would have made sure he was singing correctly, no tension on the larynx, enough breath for each pitch, forward placement of the words and then plenty of rest.

"When I was sent to Suzanne Kiechle through Karyn Robbins back in 1980 I had been writing a lot of music for film but no one would let me sing. When I first came to Suzanne, I was struggling for air and could not stay on pitch. With Suzanne's simple regimen and unique way of reconstructing the way my body 'sang' put me on a pinnacle of vocal achievement. All of a sudden I sang effortlessly with no physical strain or throat damage."

Meredith Day – Singer/Songwriter

Glossary:

Abdomen —Referring to the part of the body between the thorax and the pelvis.

Acoustic Center – Inside the mouth – the sound vibrates off the spine, cheek and jaw bones, roof of the mouth and the nose. *SK*

Ascending scale —Musical notes that go up or higher such as A,A#,B,C,C#,D

Breath – Air that is inhaled and exhaled.

Choreography - The art of creating and arranging dances

Consonant – A speech sound produced by partially or completely obstructing the flow of air from the mouth.

Cords – The vocal bands or folds that vibrate to make sound.

Cricoid cartilage – Pertaining to a ring shaped cartilage at the lower part of the larynx.

Diaphragm – The muscle separating the thoracic cavity from the abdominal cavity.

Endoscope – Slender, tubular instrument used to examine the interior of a body cavity.

Hemorrhaged vocal folds – Burst blood vessels within the vocal folds.

Hum – To sing with closed lips, without articulating words.

Humidifier – A device for increasing the amount of water vapor in the air.

Hydration – Moisture for the nasal passage: steam or saline solution for the nose, prescription or a nasal salve from your Doctor. Drinking water and hydrating liquids without acid components will hydrate. *SK*

Hyoid bone – U shaped bone at the root of the tongue.

Impediment – Obstruction, hindrance, or obstacle.

Laryngitis – Inflammation of the larynx

Larynx – Muscular and cartilaginous structure lined with mucous membrane at the upper part of the trachea – in which the vocal cords are located.

Muscle memory – Repeated, habitual muscular behavior. In singing, if the behavior is incorrect, with forced muscle movement without enough breath, can cause vocal damage. *SK*

Musculature – The muscles of the body.

Myologist – Scientist specializing in the branch of anatomy dealing with muscles.

Nasal airway – Nasal cavity.

Nodes – A blister on the vocal folds, a wearing and negative pressure on the edge of the vocal fold. In my experience, caused by tension on the larynx because there is not enough breath on certain pitches or tension on the back of the tongue from the forming of words or adjusting the pitch with the musculature of the tongue rather than using the breath. *SK*

Nose – Functions with the mouth as the usual passageway for air in respiration. It is a prominence in the center of the face formed of bone and cartilage that serves to modify or modulate the voice.

Oral cavity – The mouth.

Otorhinolaryngologist- Doctor or the ear, nose, larynx and throat.

Palpate – To examine by touch.

Pitch – To set a particular pitch or determine the key or keynote of a melody.

Reverberation – A re-echoed sound.

Soft palate – The posterior muscular portion of the roof of the mouth.

Speech pathologist – One who studies and treats the deviations from healthy or normal speech.

Stamina – Strength of physical constitution.

Syllable – A segment of speech typically produced with a single pulse of air pressure from the lungs.

Tension – The act of stretching or straining.

Throat – The passage from the mouth to the stomach or to the lungs, including the fauces, pharynx, esophagus, larynx and trachea.

TMJ – Temporomandibular joint and muscle disorders. Refers to a complex and poorly understood set of conditions that can cause pain in the area of the jaw joint and associated muscles and/or problems using the jaw.

Tone – Vocal sound made by vibrating muscular bands in the larynx, the way of sounding, modulation or intonation of the voice as expressive of meaning, feeling, spirit, etc.

Tongue – The highly mobile muscle in the floor of the mouth that facilitates speech.

Track (record) – Recorded instrumental accompaniment.

Vibrato – A pulsating effect, produced in singing by the rapid reiteration of emphases on a tone.

Vocal cords –Either of the two pairs of folds of mucous membrane projecting into the cavity of the larynx.

Vocal folds – "true" vocal cords.

Vocal tracts – The area from the laryngeal structure, spine of the neck and the entire oral cavity. *SK*

Vowels – A speech sound produced without occluding, diverting, or obstructing the flow of air from the lungs.

Yawn – To open the mouth involuntarily with a prolonged, deep inhalation of air. FOR SINGING: The **yawn** is lifting the soft palate essential for singing high notes, "making space" for the sound to come up and over. *SK*

*SK *Definitions specific to vocal training as used by Suzanne Kiechle*

> *"Suzanne is not only the greatest vocal coach in the world, she is an incredible friend. My voice has grown over the years because of her love, dedication and support of the voice, heart and soul."*
>
> *Jennifer Crestol – International Recording Artist*
> *(London Symphony)*

About the Author:
Suzanne Kiechle

Suzanne Kiechle is an internationally renowned voice teacher and vocal coach. She developed her vocal technique while working with otorhinolaryngologist Dr. Charles Schneider, who trained her in vocal physiology. Ms. Kiechle has over 34 years experience in vocal rehabilitation for singers and speakers with the following conditions: vocal nodes, chronic hoarseness, vocal fatigue, hemorrhaged vocal folds, paralyzed folds, and post-operative repair.

Her musical journey began in a home full of music and song. Her mother and two sisters all sang around the house and in the church choir. Her love of music led her to choosing an instrument – first the guitar, and then trumpet. Soon she was playing solo trumpet in the Los Angeles Junior Philharmonic conducted by Ernst Katz.

In High School Suzanne was greatly influenced by choral conductor, Lucienne Biggs, a passionate French woman who gave her a love of singing in the choir. After graduation she attended the Music Academy of the West in Santa Barbara where she studied with Master Teachers Maestro Maurice Abravanel, Julliard's David Shumann, and Martial Singher, from Curtis Institute in Philadelphia. In Mr. Singher's Master Classes, Suzanne learned to love Opera and Leider because of the connection of voice and drama in musical material. *"The observers in the audience were on the edge of their seats watching how he (Martial Singher) used small movements of the body and took the performance to new heights not often seen in Opera. It was a more subtle but very effective approach rather than the exaggerated movement typical in Operatic performances of that era. Connecting the intent, the drama and the humor with the sound of the voice was magic and it has always been a part of how I hear and see a singing performance."*

Suzanne's musical performing continued under the direction of Richard Knox and his Concert Choir, Madrigals and Jazz band with Dr. Immel. Her interest in the development of music through instruments continued with Music History teacher Dr. Catalyne who taught her to listen to every instrument in the orchestra.

A Music Scholarship to Mount St. Mary's College in Los Angeles led to a Bachelor of Music. During her college years Suzanne played the trumpet in the orchestra with Manual Compinski as conductor, and sang in the choirs with Paul Salamuovich as conductor, studied organ, piano and then studied voice outside of the school with Dr. Dean Verhines. Her final thesis was a Cantata on Peace. Paul Salamunovich conducted the Mt.St.Mary's chorus and Loyola University Chorus –with Jeannine Wagner and Alicia Rodriguez as soloists. Ms. Kiechle played one of the three trumpets. *"It was a very exciting thing to hear what you have written performed with the quality of talent I was fortunate to have for this auspicious occasion."*

Suzanne taught guitar for 13 years and was Chairman of the Music Department at Bellarmine-Jefferson High School in Burbank, California. She spent several years as a choral Conductor and Musical Director for concerts and musicals such as *"Music Man," "The Boyfriend," "Bye Bye Birdie," "Guys and Dolls," "L'il Abner," "Godspell," "Once Upon A Mattress,"* and *"Girl Crazy."*

She has been coach for TV and Movie personalities in projects such as: "Elf," "Once Upon A Mattress," "Assassination of Jesse James," the Janis Joplin Project with Zooey Deschanel, "Bones" with Emily Deschanel, "Man Trouble" with Ellen Barkin and Veronica Cartwright, "The Pirate Movie," Jimmie Rodgers Project with Matthew Modine, Bob Hope Special, "Under the Tuscan Sun"- (the boy soprano, Christopher Ibenhardt, in the wedding scene), and Monster House with Sam Lerner and Mitchell Mussso (for screaming and boys vocal change).

Suzanne works with anyone who shares her passion for singing. Her students can be seen performing throughout the world. She was guest speaker at the University of Maryland and honored at the White House as a Distinguished Teacher.

Suzanne's intention is to simplify the science of vocal production to act as a guide for professional singers, speakers, voice teachers, and choral conductors, and anyone who wants to sing and speak freely.

ACKNOWLEDGMENTS

Dr. Charles Schneider, Otorhinolaryngologist, was the one who gave me the Keys He believed in me before I believed in myself. He taught me what I know about the vocal structures, the care, the areas that are vulnerable to misuse. He first taught me how to fix my own injured vocal folds, when I had nodes. I thank you Dr. Schneider from the bottom of my heart for all the time you gave me. What you have taught me has changed my life's work.

Barbara Greene, Oral Myologist, for teaching me how truly powerful the working of the tongue is and how tongue exercises can change a malformed face to a normal face. For me this was key in my understanding of the effects of the tongue on pitch and how its misuse can cause vocal damage. Thank you, Barbara, for sharing your immense expertise of the oral cavity and the function of the tongue.

Dr. Claire O'Neill, a Chiropractor, taught me about the neck, the area of the spine connected to the vocal folds. Injuries like whiplash or more severe accidents can affect the spine which in turn can affect the working of the vocal folds. Alignment is a word used in Chiropractic and it is an important word in terms of posture and support of the voice.

Dr. Ruth McKernan, my first editor, for her encouragement and help in organizing my book in its early stages.

Jayme Goldstein, who also helped in editing and putting some order from my MAC to pages in a binder.

Katy Kerris, who is a writer and editor, took the information and pared it down to a user friendly document and put structure to the book. Katy understands the subject and my intent as a voice teacher to be clear and specific about vocal production. Katy is a singer and an Occupational Therapist, who understands it from both perspectives, vocally and medically. Katy is good at keeping me in check so I don't get too redundant. God bless you Katy, for offering to help put my life's work in book form.

Barbara Weatherwax, my friend for 50 years, who is an author herself and artist and singer, knows how to do it all and she understands and encourages my creative self to give all I can to this book. How very blessed I am to have Barbara work with me on this book and bring it to life.

John Bowdler, bless his soul, is my tech support. Thank you John for all your help with my computer and all its functions. He is "Johnny" on the spot when I get freaked out and can't get things to work in the tech zone.

Special Thanks to:

Paul Kerris, for his expert drawing of the side view of the head, tongue and larynx.

Heidi Uhl, for taking the pictures that illustrate the physical positions.

Paula Kerris, for proofreading and helping me to make last minute decisions.

A teacher must first be a student . I thank my many teachers especially *Paul Salamunovich*, for imparting musical knowledge, singing on the breath, linear phrasing, keeping the sound moving forward, and the inner beat of the music which adds to the life of the sound. He helped me experience the beauty in Choral singing. He often talked about sound, how to get all these different voices to blend and to emotionally arc together. Mr. Salamunovich has been an inspiration to me for many years.

No teacher can do a job without the most important people, the students. They inspire me to communicate my knowledge and I am very lucky to have students who are passionate about singing. I thank ALL of my students past and present for being partners with me in the journey to the **Keys To Vocal Freedom.**